Puffins Climb, Penguins Rhyme

WRITTEN AND PHOTO-ILLUSTRATED BY Bruce McMillan

VOYAGER BOOKS / HARCOURT, INC.

San Diego   New York   London

Puffins land.

Puffins stand.

Penguins groom.

Penguins zoom.

Puffins fly.

Puffins lie.

Penguins nest.

Penguins rest.

Puffins meet.

Puffins eat.

Penguins stare.

Penguins care.

Puffins walk.

Puffins squawk.

Penguins brawl.

Penguins call.

Puffins hear.

Puffins peer.

Penguins glare.

Penguins share.

Puffins hide.

Puffins glide.

Penguins clean.

Penguins preen.

Puffins see.

Puffins flee.

Penguins hop.

Penguins stop.

Heimaklettur, Heimaey Island, Iceland

Atlantic puffins
(Fratercula arctica arctica)

live at the top of the world.

Atlantic puffins:

live in the Northern Hemisphere where summer occurs from June to September.

grow to a height of about 10 inches (25 centimeters).

all (males and females) have identical plumage and colors.

lose the bright colors of their bill, face, legs, and feet for winter.

can fly as fast as 50 miles per hour (82 kilometers/hour).

make underwater dives — as long as 33 seconds — to catch small fish to eat.

can dive to depths of about 147 feet (45 meters).

propel themselves underwater by beating their wings.

steer underwater by using their feet as rudders.

migrate annually, living far at sea most of the year.

only come ashore during the spring and summer.

nest during the spring and summer.

usually dig an underground tunnel or find a rock cavern for a nesting burrow in which to lay eggs.

usually lay one egg per mating pair of puffins each season.

feed their chicks tiny whole fish.

shed their feathers every year at the end of the winter while at sea.

cannot fly until new feathers have grown in.

Southern gentoo penguins

(Pygoscelis papua ellsworthii)

live at the bottom of the world.

Port Lockroy, Wiencke Island, Antarctica

Southern gentoo penguins:

live in the Southern Hemisphere where summer occurs from December to February.

grow to a height of about 30 inches (76 centimeters).

all (males and females) have identical plumage and colors.

keep the same bill and feather colors all year long.

cannot fly.

make underwater dives — as long as 2 minutes — to catch mostly krill, a shrimplike animal, to eat.

can dive to depths of about 492 feet (150 meters).

propel themselves underwater by beating their wings (which are usually called flippers).

steer underwater by using their feet as rudders.

appear not to migrate, spending most of their time near their nest area.

usually come ashore all year round.

nest during the spring and summer.

build an exposed, bowl-shaped nest of small rocks in which to lay eggs.

usually lay two eggs per mating pair of penguins each season.

feed their chicks regurgitated food of partially digested krill or squid.

shed their feathers every year at the end of summer while ashore.

cannot swim until new feathers have grown in.

For "Mr. A,"
John Anagnostis,
my Kennebunk High School English teacher

The photographs on pages 5 and 28 appeared in *Penguins at Home:
Gentoos of Antarctica*, copyright © 1993 by Bruce McMillan.

www.harcourt.com

First Voyager Books edition 2001
Voyager Books is a trademark of Harcourt, Inc.,
registered in the United States of America and other jurisdictions.

The Library of Congress has cataloged the hardcover edition as follows:
McMillan, Bruce.
Puffins climb, penguins rhyme/written and photo-illustrated by Bruce McMillan.
p. cm.
1. Puffins—Juvenile literature. 2. Penguins—Juvenile literature. [1. Puffins. 2. Penguins.] I. Title.
QL696.C42M395 1995
598.3'3—dc20 94-27225
ISBN 0-15-200362-2
ISBN 0-15-202443-3 pb

E F G H

The photographs in this book were shot with Nikon F4/MF23 or FE2 cameras mounted with 24, 50, 105, 300,
or 600 mm lenses, using Kodachrome 64 Professional film processed by Kodalux.
The maps were drawn in India ink by the author/photo illustrator.
The display and text type were set in Neuzeit by Thompson Type, San Diego, California.
Printed and bound by Tien Wah Press, Singapore
Production supervision by Sandra Grebenar and Ginger Boyer
Designed by Bruce McMillan and Camilla Filancia

A Note from the Author

Puffins Climb, Penguins Rhyme provides a visit to both polar regions. The puffins and penguins were photographed within 250 miles of the Arctic and Antarctic circles, respectively. I photographed the puffins on Heimaey Island off the southern coast of Iceland in May, June, and August 1993. The penguins were photographed along the Antarctic Peninsula in January and February 1992. The puffin trips to Iceland were made possible in part by Einar Gustavsson and the Iceland Tourist Board, and the penguin expeditions to Antarctica by Travel Dynamics. I am also indebted to my Icelandic friend, Kristján Egilsson, director of the Museum of Natural History and Aquarium in Vestmannaeyjar, for his invaluable help.

The verbs in this book describe bird behavior, though the open-billed "squawk" may not result in what many readers are expecting — sound. The puffin "squawk" is a soundless squawk of intimidation. Puffins often gape open their bills to inform a nearby puffin that an area is temporarily taken. Though this squawk is silent, puffins can and do vocalize. In cliffside burrows they hum a soft *rrrrrh-rrrrrh-rrrrrh*, similar to the motorlike sound that cats make when they purr. But if puffins nest in the echo chamber of a rock-crevice burrow, the same *rrrrrh-rrrrrh-rrrrrh* sounds like a muffled miniature chainsaw. The puffin hum is very different from the loud penguin "call," *ah-ahaa-ahaa-aheeee!* The donkey-sounding penguin bray can be heard up to a half-mile from the source.

This book introduces children to the behavior of two amusing birds that live in remote places. It also introduces children to a playful form of two-word minimalist poetry that I call verb verse. Simple, two-word rhyming sentences consisting of a repeating noun and a one-syllable verb, matched with photos that provide visual word clues, help beginning readers to recognize and learn unfamiliar words. I hope this book inspires in all readers, young and old, an appreciation of our natural world and its inhabitants — and that the simple rhymes inspire young readers to create their own verb verses.

Bruce McMillan